T0162494

Crabwise to the Hounds

Jeramy Dodds

Coach House Books | Toronto

Published with the generous assistance of the Canada Council for the Arts and the Ontario Arts Council. Coach House Books also acknowledges the support of the Government of Ontario through the Ontario Book Publishing Tax Credit Program and the Government of Canada through the Book Publishing Industry Development Program.

LIBRARY AND ARCHIVES CANADA CATALOGUING IN PUBLICATION

Dodds, Jeramy, 1974-
Crabwise to the hounds / Jeramy Dodds. -- 1st ed.

Poems.
ISBN 978-1-55245-205-9

I. Title.

PS8607.O396C73 2008   C811'.6   C2008-904261-1

to
Josh,
Leigh
& Gabe

Give yourself up to Remote Control.
There is no choice, either you come knowing
or not knowing. You come.
      – Christopher Dewdney

DRY HEART

A bed
robbed of its river.
A derelict hornet's nest,

Japanese paper. Whistling
with a mouth full of crackers.
Cotton-swabbed, book-pressed,

museumed. Passed out
naked in the sun. Embalmed.
Powder in a fluorescent bulb.

Coral in a souvenir shop.
Lathe and plaster.
Vermouth. The roof

of an umbrella's mouth,
vacuum sacks of dandruff,
gunpowder.

Sixteenth-century German furniture.
Hot-air balloon.

Ash.

It was the year I subscribed to an absurd
number of magazines. There were lions everywhere.
Lions at the tambourines, lions in the gatehouse, lions
up the sleeve of your bible-black dress, you could set your watch
by the screams, the shimmy-shackle of claws
on the hardwood floor wore down your ear, ghosts
of lions fathered our kids, lions of the long grass,
Barnum & Bailey types, we knelt at the scimitar scar
on the tamer's breast as valets brought lions upon lions,
lions going at us with the violence of a clearance sale, my wife
comes home with a lion between her legs, antelope musk
hog-tied in her mouth, bed-lamp–bright wounds,
a yoke of tear-jars tingling from her nicked shoulders,
lions cornered in her cranium, the wedding dancers slain,
their scattered organs like gobs of fruit, lions
at the chink in our *amour*, lions on the owls, lions
like Labs, the house pets snapped, lions loaded for bear,
lions at the crypt ledger jotting down kills,
plaster casts of claws above our cancer-ward doors, lions
parted the curtains of our ribs, panted like whistling arrows,
starved lions, hair painted on their bones,
lions in the yard with the kids, lions
at the midnight fridge, chicken on their lips,
lions at the watering hole bullying
for beer money, lions mowing through
the Foot Guard, Beefeaters, Dragoons,
standing in perfect pecking order
at my bedside, waiting for me to snap
the bones of my watch to my wrist
and dress in their gift of slipper-thin armour.

HEIMLICH

Comes up behind you at a party, masks your eyes
with his mammogram hands, asks, 'Guess who?'
A bear-hugger from way back. Trains by wrapping
around bridge pilings, vending machines, a Douglas fir.
Avoided at most parties: too clingy, too close a talker.
Hovers near buffet trays glaring at your chest, hands
rasping between songs. You poke fun at his tight
lederhosen, his tin flute, but you've bitten off
more than you can chew. Through the crowd
he rushes to you, binds two fists into one under
your sternum. By his second squeeze, the ghosts
of mine canaries flood your mouth and stream
to that part of horizon he's left ajar.

PROSTHETICS

*Despite all the amputations you know you could just go out
and dance to the rock and roll stations, and it was all right.*
— *Lou Reed*

I'm on the pier with my back against
the wrecking machine. Cyclones of terns
turn atop prop-churned debris.
This morning I feel like the wheel
you fell asleep at. Godstruck by the flag
clotted on its pole like the skin of a starved
animal. The downcoast ferry's
run out of hearing. A spaghetti-strap dress,
a trembling gin, as you shift weight
to your wooden leg.

Ear to a conch, I hear
acrobats in waiting rooms
flipping through magazines,
the gull squawk of the guitarist's hand
going to chord, stunt men falling
through awning after awning.
The sea is a soliloquy
in a buried warehouse.

But March is the month of swollen doors.
Boots bark through checkerweaves of ice.
Lacking prophylactics, we pull apart
to watch our dead sons run along your one
good leg. Hitting the deck, they hoist dust
to their meniscus shoulders.

The sea, a surface unworn by our movement.
Our shore leave, a landscape painted
with a brush made
from the hair of the dog
of those storm-closed roads,
as though a gale had come to town
and left wearing pelicans.

Down the orchard ladder our Emissaries came.
They had been letting the sea do their laundry.
They had been sentenced to bear false witness.
Part the blinds and the sun guillotines.
Pull them, and light chokes back its lure.
Bigger than any country music legend.
Brighter than a birdroom for stars.

Down the orchard ladder our Emissaries came.
With a taxidermist's jar of glass eyes.
With the underwater wind of riptides.
Part my low-lying lap-pleated hands.
Pull my hair back.
Bigger than a blind man's once-over.
Badder than sailors home from their maroon.

Down the orchard ladder our Emissaries came.
Afterwards my armhairs lay like floodgrass.
Aftermath is the sum of nothing but the facts.
Part my seeing into staying and leaving.
Pull the chute on my left-leaning heart.
Record the euthanists rehearsing.
Mic the trapeze snap.

Down the orchard ladder our Emissaries came.
In the household of their cupped hands
are the rivers we ransomed.
In the pits along their mantrap lines
are the acrobats we let go.
Part the flaming bulrushes, the sunken river sticks.
Pull yourself together, because our Emissaries have come

down the aluminum rungs we sawed
half through, and they're standing,
wearing *I'm with Stupid* T-shirts
beside you.

THE SHOWER CAPER

I had come to brush my teeth.
You had been in here for some time,
standing in the corner shower.
Splay of toothpaste speckling the mirror
with constellations, snowpoints.
The water circles above the drain,
brings its buffaloes to the cliffs.
Your toes squint on the lime stains
left from the pouncing of the taps.
I missed you turning to me,
or maybe you didn't, hands up
on the shower wall as if some water-cops
had you frisked. And me moving in
to interrogate just as they
were beading away.

> *Deer, a jackrabbit the size of a motorcycle.*
>   *– Tim Lilburn*

Hit quick, the road-wasted stag
fell like the sick sorrel horse
we hunted by syringe
in a 3 x 5 pen. His fallen
figure-skater sprawl
drew out our awe, lying
on his own canvas of blood,
iron tailings from a ran-down mill.
Overcoated men with leather bags
of tinctures and bitters
couldn't bring him around.
Witnesses stood, arms crossed,
afraid their hands might reach
for the debris of muscle guyropes
knifed by the blunt bumper of an suv.
Looking aside I saw
a young woman come out
of the woods and work
her way through the crowd,
coming to rest in a kneel
at the buck's breast.
We moved to halt her
but she heeled us with one hand
while the other slid to his snapped
sapling crown. She rubbed her fingers
gently down his brow, grappling his snout
to bring his half-yard of neck right round.

SOUND ADVICE

Uncontrolled air traffic cussing
like a bar parrot above our heads,
rope walkers hauling nets full
of cicadas, a bed race on cobble
streets, a band check-checking,
a man running with a gut full
of rain, a falcon flailing
in the recovery wing of the aviary,
a Halifax harbour alarm clock
waking you with the sound of holding down
a job like reaching into a snare drum
and having to chew off your arm to escape
the rhythm of rain touching a tight tarp,
bush wolves downing deer, an ant
lost in brain coral, teens jeering a moth
bucked by the porch bulb's heat,
the first motor on a morning lake,
a ghetto blaster belting from a bandshell,
someone crying *breakfast* at the whitecap
of your wet dream, gutting the mind
like a house on fire.

BOOGALOO

At every fête,
when the ass of a balloon opens,
we follow its tune, for whoever
that failing balloon brushes
becomes immune to voodoo.

You and whose doll, I knew not,
walked the churchyard then stopped
to cram a hairpin into its burlap.
I did not fold, but someone somewhere
cupped his loins.

We are only allowed to live
due to some colossal misunderstanding.
In rec rooms across this land
perpetual galas rage, throngs
of ball-gowned survivalists
scan skyward, arms spread
for breath-propelled balloons
that lap pristine ceilings.

Or until our effigies of each other drop
tears that teem like a sea of chandeliers.

SQUARE GRAND PIANO, CIRCA 1880

A lip skirmish near the water closet
set the parlour ablaze. Parting ways,
one teatime talker, a noted tiger hunter,
confessed to the slingshot-wounded waiter
that he had torn the cranberry cap of a scab
from his Russian mail-order bride's knee while
getting a dustpan for the saucer she broke
over the brow of gravity. Boys, did it bleed, did it
drizzle. The way he talked about her would make
your shins splint. She held records in the biathlon;
she dressed in poufs, swags and drapes; her first night
in our teak-trimmed opera house was consummated
by pitch-perfect castratos fingering the ebonies,
all pinkies and damper pedal. And you know
what they say: snow is rosin dust off the violinist's bow.
Beyond the whale-lard lamps we watched the high-bred help
swallow the key to the door of the outbuilding where
the hill-whiskey was housed. Mules reared. Rabbits ate themselves
blind. We were left alone to pickle any oddity, to be Victorians.
There we were then, at the crest of our epoch. All clash,
all scramble. From the widow's walk I watched the last
lighthousekeeper put his daughter to bed before jumping
from the torch to deaden the fold of a stray wave.

This is all we knew when the Longcoats arrived,
and one of them, their leader perhaps, moved
from the fold as Job's tears stood parched
on the windowsill and a barren corn crib
slanted in the back lot. You tend to take it
twenty-fold, the image of music. Sitting
at the black bench he made the piano tumble,
tumble like a trebuchet-shot aquanaut
piercing the spine of horizon.

HAPPY BIRTHDAY, CARL LINNAEUS, 300 YEARS OLD

Linnaeus was only 154 cm tall.
But he cut an impressive figure
when clad in his Sami costume,
as he did when he proposed to Sara Lisa.
Furthermore, he had beautiful eyes.
Linnaeus was the first European
to successfully cultivate bananas.
He managed this while living in Holland.
Linnaeus claimed that the forbidden fruit
Eve offered Adam in the Garden of Sweden
was a banana. Linnaeus wrote texts
that were easy to understand. Linnaeus's
speculations became bolder as he became older.
For example: he speculated that swallows
spent the winter at the bottom of lakes.
Maybe he was in a hurry to explain things.

Out of the morass he looked like
a reconstructed grenade. Pelt burdened
by burrs. Corroded cloak pin of his cant-hook claws.
The bulrushes gave their windhead nods.
At his lope, spores backstep and scatter.
And that spine scar where the key enters and winds.
The beehive of his eyes sends droids to probe
the switchgrass. So still, the windsocks
hung like daggered lungs. His bible is a flipbook
of practical anatomy. His sightline, a river
you can't talk across. An inmate running his tin cup
along the bars is the muscle-headed bruise racing
inside his ribs like a motorbike in a cage ball.
From southern cape to southern cape
his lungs are a harrow's width apart.
His cochlea is a spoon-dug tunnel beneath
the pet cemetery, his saphenous nerve, a boy
with a bouquet of fresh horses. His irises are owls
and owls are cached hunks of bonfire soot.
His hunger strike does not include giving up fellatio.
Veins are a Gorgon's black-adder bouffant.
Capillaries are winter maples scrubbing the mist.
Blood cells are dust-taxied down a flashlight's path.
His mouth is my mother crying in the car wash.
Dew-worm hunters hatch kerosene lamps
on the gospel choir of his brain
while he comes crawling in his Sunday best,
as though his spine were a bell rope
at midnight and the village vacant
and his father had gone to town
with his inheritance – an Alsatian
that was a dowry for the distance
he'd cross day after dawn after dusk.

22

Yank your habit from the hat,
temper-tap it on the rump, tell it,
naughty little bastard. There he is
at the tail of a trail of look-alike
chocolate-covered raisins, that's him,
the effin' ticker of his clock pounding,
teasing Alice through a haze, just to dry-hump
her shiny shoe. Near dawn he's at a cabbage grab
in your English garden. Tell him what we do
to thieves in this town: lop off that unlucky foot,
that sawdust-stuffed necromancer, perpetually on point,
teeth tocking to his jackalope cousin while wolves
tear through the kitchen, he jigs in the tall grass
when St. Jean's head is lopped into a whisker basket.
In your child's room, Bunnicula sits fanged
in a chicken-wire cage. Not a good idea
to set him on your lap, heavy-pet his ears back,
better let him drown in the well of a hat,
next to the tricks we've done
when we're all thumbs.

A theremin quartet backed
by ventilation-shaft singers,
a score staged for the shadow theatre,
piano-bar piano music
that reminds us the moon lip-syncs
the sun. A brushed drum like *help*
snuffed in a rag-stuffed mouth,
the velvet pit of your mouth
on my mouth last November.
Pale and bedded on a tasselled
rag duvet, we are cautious,
as though calling a stranger's
dog. In the painting over our heads
a hound hauls a gored goose
like a rose in its teeth through the reeds
to his gunman. That same gunman's
in the room next to ours, propped
on two pillows, sucking
a cigarette red, humming the chorus
full bore, flat out.

THE CASUAL MATADOR

At one point, while I'm deep in sleep,
she goes for water.

The lake is unpinned and sloshes in its bowl,
what weather radio calls *a front*.

I wake and, thinking she's gone for good,

totter on the edge of bed
like a bull
full of swords.

HIRAM BINGHAM

*In 1912, the modest Mr. Bingham stumbled on Machu Picchu
while surveying the local jungle with his crew.*

A slog through the faunal farm, pushing
a savvy squad of mules, goading pack-boys
with the promised payment of the sleek slit
of a woman. Tactically sulking, his lips' chasm
gaps only to scold: 'You there, get on or we'll
never find her, and who would we be then?'

The tent's mouth propped by a pole, he's
at the oak table brought here by ox, washed up
on the shore of a tipped tiara of lamplight,
jotting doodles of dreary dearest in the margins
of a Holstein-hide diary. Cornered in the all-talk
witchery of jungle, each floral spawn is an acute
observation tower measuring the majesty of his march.

Guilty of steering millions to the fragility of Machu
Picchu. How do you sleep with the trail boss's latinates
ransacking you for the cure for this common goal:
to have your name in brights, the thwap of your eyelids
falling down the well of every jungle drum, your
name at attention on the tips of each forked tongue?

MOORHEN

The tubas are full of fog and fallen thoroughbreds.
There are no dogs near the dentist's office
due to the pitch of the drills. A poem
is meant to replace what the olfactory erased.
But it always comes out like a Gilbert-without-
Sullivan song.

In the birdbath my reflection sprains
with each plop of rain. We don't find it odd
that mule saddles are made from cows?
But the moorhen is two birds killed
with one act of kindness.

Above all, the clouds are like tennis skirts,
fenceposts dark where dogs piss their names.
Her mouth a doily-gagged coal hole. No squawk
as my palm kowtows her gullet to the block,
her hind high for our singsong.

Now, if I tap-test the mic, and tell you all,
I'll know the cassettes of our joy are socked away
in the secret drawers of my boudoir. O you
can't tell someone just how lonely he is,
but a moorhen sure can.

VALDEMAR ATTERDAG RANSACKS VISBY, AGAIN

In his stovepipe hat, he hunted
to extinction the animals that brought
us déjà vu. The pole bore no flag
as the fragmented and tyrannical darklings
scuttled the pebble beach for the last
of our beliefs. Why then did the ruins,
rejuvenated under dawn's
sleight of hand, collapse anew?
Like a post-orgasm pervert who has
found a fresh manor of self-pleasure
in your lovely's tossed bedcloth?

Forgeries aside, I cannot comprehend
the wren, bullet-holed but breathing
still, as the ruin on which, melting,
the amber cause of our discontent
dulls in the bell's ripple and ebb.

THE OFFICIAL TRANSLATION OF HO CHI MINH'S AUGUST 18TH, 1966, TELEPHONE CALL

Tell me the windows aren't really sweating.

You should come back when I've something better to wear.

I'm sorry but no one could tell me the time
and I was worried I'd be late.

The birds are the ones pulling out the rain.

After it's all down, it makes the outdoors like a basement.

I can see the antennae are bored.

I'm tall, but not as tall as my shadow would allow.

There are no church bells, but gates
often rattle on their latches.

My favourite line in a newspaper story:
He brought up the gun and let it go.

My favourite sign:
Those likely to die on the premises are strongly discouraged.

My favourite thing about America
is the inhale sound of cars on the streets after rain.

The last time I heard her name it was breaking through my sleep.

In the sky are hills of weather.

The croissant really isn't that great.

I hear shouts and stay away from the curfewed parts of town.

I swear the garbage truck arrives earlier each week.

Before you came, I saw clouds waterfalling over the mountains.

When I'm out for dinner I never want to meet the cook;
I just don't want to know.

The front step of my aunt's house dips at its centre.

When you came, the wind drew back in.

I have seen him wandering through camp talking to his feet
as if they were a dog.

I worry about people washing their cars late at night.

I'm more worried about the way you drive
than the number of drinks you've had.

The bat-winged junks are lovingly filled with RPGs.

Things I will never hold:
the lightning on the sun, the diamonds of the sea …

*[On the tape he leaves the telephone and you can hear the sound
of latches tumbling, sheets flapping on the line, a match striking.
He coughs in the distance before returning to add:]*

If, by the time you get here, the telephone

is dangling from its carriage

and emptying into the room, it is

because I have gone outside to repair

the night through a colander of stars.

Falconers rise to seat their ravenous
debutantes. Peacocks spot-welded to
wrought-iron perches, mum's-the-word
maids and dumbwaiters refraining in a
courtyard creased by shadows cast from
astral black trees, trees bent like
threadbare umbrella bones. The glen
downwind is peppered with untethered
foals, their knees like pythons with
puffer fish in their midriffs. I arrive in
an ivory suit under the nebular nursery
of floodlights. I bow to our lady of the
mansion, then sit to splay my haymaker
hands on the peck-dulled ebonies. My
melodic bloom, a minotaur run aground
by the shatter of moon thrown from our
lady's gold-sequin shoes. Shoes you could
land biplanes by in a blanket fog, the
kind you buy an ivory horn for and keep
crated under floorboards when the
Homeguard shoulders down your door.
All night we sat on the settee and spoke
sternly to the parrots her parents kept
caged. While one wolf-bent wrist sickled
her handbag's handles, the other guided a
clay carafe to my glass –

I am shackled to a dunetop like a *tree
lightning loves*. Ten chains away
the first sprig is torn from the precious
spring storm. The lady of the mansion
stands in the bloodburst of sunrise,

her dogwood fingers holding back
a herd of frothing foals by the throats
so I could pass immaculate
over the runnels, under the polefence,
and into the arms of that gondolier
with her coinpurse pursed
for my penniless eyes.

The crabapple seeds
eventually grew through
the tongue-and-groove,
breaking the news to Father
of the spoon-dug crawlway
I hollowed below. Father's
pipe-bomb science could not
explain the landfill of clouds
in the birdbath. This land,
a crime scene of weather clues,
this bugle hack-sawed from a copper still.
This is no patter of rain painting the window
wet, this is Father revving his black Corvette
and hurtling us down oak-boughed roads
to the place where we'll winter.
And I'll rehearse in my
under-earth auditorium
audienced by buried pets.
My conductor's wand, the bough
where undead owls perch, their jowls packed
with soot, their barrelfire eyes burning
the brush-offs I gave public school chicks.
And my fingers pump those three brass pistons
while my loosed lungs sync with an ancient
score that blows the pearled gates off-hinge
and lets my Heralds spill: all my dead
pets reanimated by my alchemic music,
screeching for all our dearth,
combing the dells, dockyards
and ravishments for rumours
forsaking me since birth.

DODGE DART

I bought the car on sweet time. The farm
was sure to follow. The rear-view washing
its face in its hands as the whirl road
unrolled. The side-views like gosling wing nubs.
My girl Tonda diddling herself on the backbench
of this shatterproof sea lion tromped
and taking the long way to Sault Ste. Marie.
The mind, a somersault unable to unravel.
Summer a time when hourglass girls
arrange roadside wreaths between
the desperate restaurants. The road
remade for us upon our approach,
the coniferous part-and-reseal
after our passing, the mind splashes.
Tonda's buzzer goes when
a dead cedar marsh appears.
And if the pines weren't preoccupied
with darting and infilling, they'd correct
young Tonda: 'People don't really mean
the woods,' she sighs and dabs
her soaked brow in the rear-view
as the road buttons up
behind us. 'They just say,
"Let's go to the woods."'

CONTRAPUNCTUS

> *'There is an excellent early seventeenth-century engraving by*
> *Franz van der Wyngaert, Mr. Peterson, in which a cat-piano*
> *appears. Played, as it happens, by a man with a wooden leg.*
> *You will observe my own leg.' The cat-piano player hoisted*
> *his trousers and a leglike contraption of wood, metal and*
> *plastic appeared.*
> — *Donald Barthelme*

He tipped the forepeak of his tricorn (hounds
were tongue-to-arse in the heather), and put his
club foot down to hobble along troughs cattle had worn
in the bedrock, past lacklustre cisterns (where beekeepers
stacked a hedge of white box-hives along the field's edge).
With translucent hands he dragged the oak door open
(and put the gramophone's arm on the last leg of your
journey) to the bird-bone shack where the cat-pianos sat.

In a Vimy trench coat (his tickertape scarf in ragtime
with mahogany gusts) he stood at the upright (like
an usher) in the Palace of Breeze. His (tripwire-gashed) shin
pulled the bench leg in. His Imperial Guard (in earbud mics)
stood thigh high in the undertones. His hands (hair-triggered)
shatter (each piece of quiet), like willow-ware skeet.
His (hen-boned) feet counting (sand dollars to) dust while
the (player-piano's) Braille spool (chased its own tail) chased its
own tail. Mrs. Peterson, his (plumb-perfect) crime was to step
(beneath your dress) with a (mirror-toed) shoe, and rumba,
hands hocking (like a hound's nape) your hip's flesh. In this
(wrecker's) den he made love (to you) while widow-makers
watched. And that tall ivory-toothed music box chucked itself
(thirty-two Russian blues fast) far into your recently indecent past.

His hiatuses bloom on the kitchen's sill.
His shirt snaps like tiny animals falling
through branches. In stride with the clock's
hypnotics, his throat chops a glass of water
down.

He tugs a stone boat with his palomino team
to the birch lot's edge where silence
shipwrecks on silence.

Where deadfall tangoes with live trees,
like botflies on cowbacks, bird shadows
fleck the rye. Tomorrow he'll pen and shear
the last-but-not-leasts. And all winter sing,
'I'll not go missing on that river.'

North of lumberless land,
we made the animals fight for us.
Sore warped beasts pinched off
the rag-and-bone rack, ones that
bit by barbed bit were forced to
fisticuffs in the scrub slump of hills.
With a hairline rapture these animals
came and went about our days,
leaving their young to defend
the palaces they were forced from
for us. These carousel mammals walked
skewered to the pole. With forepaws
in kid gloves they pricked ears when
tinder sticks lapped the brass-green
kettledrums, drums that laid down the miles
to their relevant demise.

After rock-picking, the fields
were pocked. My uncle with a hazel switch
kicking his mule's hide. My uncle
after twenty more one-mores, his
hat-hidden forehead facing hindsight
as he ox-eyed the ten-ton dewline
that girdled the drumlins. His
cat-o'-nine-tailed spine
humped along the timber-slab paths,
his blinkered mule craning at the headlands;
his pelt hides bone anchor points, marrow levers,
sanguine pulleys. An oilcloth dropped
on his doily-thin, God-given name.

And that's our house, dog-eared
by a balepick hooked in the gatepost
like a tongue licked on winter tin. From
a Caesarean cloudbelly, grey hounds of rain
tear messenger pigeons down to half-tilled fallow.
From the crown of the fox tower I pull my scope
from its rat-hide case, come in close on Uncle,
that mule under his loins scraping home
in ankle drags. The gully was as far as I got
by eye. The rest I only heard,
the noise I'm writing to forget
as the barren hounds got onto him.

moves to the beat of door security
patting you down. But once inside
the brass mansionlands, the first thing
you'll notice is that all the sunners
have left for the night. Their towels
on the beach are the casket flags
we brought the dead home beneath.
Here trees eat their young.
When Laura died I dropped everything
and could only crawl for a month.
The birch is a perilous porcelain machine.
Lowering her and her heirlooms below
the limestone, the last she could see
through the gaps in the knit of her veil:
a peregrine, the moraine, a ruined horse.

In Lhasa, she canned her Sherpas on the steep, and with
her own bone frame bent by lament, advertised anew:

Been hoping for a gold-rush senator
third removed from a tsar, counterclockwise

to the steeplechase, a media hound,
a lackey bagboy moonlighting monthly,

blue as a skink, strong as a morning cock
shod of his spurs and ready to carry the load.

No Parisian purse-snatcher or crick-back
alarm-clock dinger. His voice must be like

snowploughs finding pavement,
arms like a buckled train, waterbed thighs –

mutt lineage aside, he must be bulldoggish
but with hands so soft paper could stop them.

PIN-UP

On the most beautiful day for air strikes
she's spread-eagled on a funereal loveseat
like a memorial to a lost airliner.

That belle of the Armistice Ball
left our whole division gut-punched
when she drove off in our memorabilia.
Our squadron ace pulling her from under
his barrack mattress as, minute by minute,
the machine-gun nests cried to be fed.
Sirens wrung like soaked rags over the base
as our curtain calls for her rang like a telephone
in a house where no one's home.

The one thing fallen airmen always recall
is the reflection of her tiny pornographer,
in his cricket clothes, caught in the funhouse mirror
of the kitchen kettle's chrome. How he clasped her
in the clink of his shutter, so careful to keep from us
the dewlaps of a monarch, on a sprig
of baby's breath, in the corner
of those thighs she just untied.

Over there.
Windmills. Wheat.
Where?
Piebald sky. Pitch.
The other side
of the river.
Deergod. Crop-slap.
Wet mares. Amok.
Shemp's bridge
is just ahead.
Flintlocks. Cocked.
There.
A raze. Guncrash.
Got one!
Stars. Look.
Saltshot.
Where'd they …
Paw-bat. *Whap.*
<*Gasp*>
Hackletracks.
Jon, get up a tree …
Muddotted.
Cinchstrap.
Jon. Jon?
Birch. Birch.
Moon.

Shipwrights shoulder-pole
bedrolls and Swede-saws
through a cellophane of rain.
Rent boys pony up to door frames
as cliff-dwellers stare down
dead holes in the sun. Cocklers
chase the tide on oxcarts through
a dogbreath of fog, the only surviving
automobile whitewashed black
by the coal era. Pit-fire plumes
cockeyed by bugling black gulls
who three-toe on the paunches
of our dead. Every night watchfires
unshadow piles of gun-felled fawns
by a river that roars like silverware drawers
poured on the rocks. Insect voyeurs infest
every weather-heckled clapboard house.
They come through lugholes and dog-scratched
screen doors. In the hilltop hospitals, gurney-ridden men
sob the names of make-believe seas as nurses hustle
like hummingbirds at the underside of their elbows.
In the maternity ward, a young astral projectionist lies
like a stillborn, though he's old enough to know better,
as his appledoll elders, with their skirt-smothered legs,
go forth daily to stone the crows. His dream twitches
scrub starshine from the bedsheets.
In a courtyard of hem-scuffed stone,
he appears to charade sandstorms
and sea surges until night backslides and
lamps are pinched out between spit-soaked
fingers, clouds like night nurses
with pillows drawn tight between
their fists. In the snuffed morn

the lighthousekeeper's only daughter
appears in his bedchamber's door frame
with poached game on her hands,
her milk-bowl glare tied like mules' cargo
to the buckled oak floor when he offers,
'The sea's lid is a million sighs wide
and this, my dear, is where I tell you how
your husband drowns.'

VENTRILOQUIST DUMMIES

For four days my cardigan reeked
from the flurry of their applause.
That sign-language opera,
the fat lady of my life.

But after each shtick
he open-palms my freckled
cheek, *You little shit.*

He hoists me to the balcony
in an electrical storm –
my arms raised to the lintel, looking
like timber cologned with gas,
hearing a match.

His finger, a gun
in the back of my mind
whenever I ad lib, and he sees
it's *me* they guffaw for.

I had the nerve to conduct the impulse. Fashioned
a deep-space craft of haywired rebar, papier mâché,
crocheted twine walls, fibreglassed in and finished
with pan-flat soup cans to shingle the hull; built to be
dire fast, opening earth's postcard weather
to ghost in the tar pot of space.

Without proper protective clothing, I step into my oven-mitt
jumpsuit, a cardigan covered by buttons, a milk-jug husk
helmet, an artificial-palm-frond cloak. Donning my yard-sale
Aqua Lung, I wheel the dimmer switch wide. Freon-cooled boosters
seethe and lambaste the turret of my broken home into the silo
that tossed my dark craft: a pommel horse turned electric bull
turned intergalactic claptrap.

But a week out, bored shitless, all the vodka on board drunk,
pissed out, drunk again, I wanted to get back to where
I once belonged. I ham-radioed for days, *Please*.
On the seventh day, a craft seersucked from the deaf stars,
a one-piece seamless number, whose tractor beam
grabbed my port-side fin – the hoist point – the ear
I was brought back home by.

THE EASIEST WAY TO EMPTY A SEASHELL
IS TO PLACE IT ON AN ANTHILL

> *Don't be frightened. Mr. Gould is here, he will appear*
> *in a moment. I am not, as you know, in the habit of speaking*
> *on any concert except the Thursday night previews, but a*
> *curious situation has arisen which merits, I think, a word*
> *or two. We are about to hear a rather, shall we say,*
> *unorthodox performance of the Brahms D Minor Concerto,*
> *a performance distinctly different from any I've ever heard,*
> *or even dreamt of for that matter…*
> > *– Leonard Bernstein introducing Glenn Gould playing*
> > *the Brahms D Minor Concerto Op. 15, April 9, 1962,*
> > *New York*

At first his right and left hands hover over the keys
before falling to the ivory
like a luggage-bombed Boeing.

His right hand on the trebles moving
at the rate it takes to stitch shut
the eyes of a hawk.

Left hand low and slow, corking
scraps of breath in perfume bottles.

His right is a palace revolution,
the King's own gave them the keys.

Left hand like an ancient fish that has come
to enjoy long walks on the beach.

His right, lucky as finding a duffle of porn
the day after his girlfriend left.

His left, like drilling rain
pocking the pond before resting

like a cowboy in a hip bath,
smoking a cigar in front of the fire.

Meanwhile, his right walks like a woman
entering a dry stone hut knuckled on a hill,

her wounded revolutionary lying inside. She
carries a basket of bread covered with a towel.

His left makes the rich nervous.

His right skis to the North Star, seeing-eye dog of explorers.

His left pivots at the star and stumbles in perfect harmony
like an actor playing the Bullet-Riddled Man.

His right is under oath.

His left's careful as a cobweb in a dry sink.

His right practices the foolproof rhythm method.

His left starts a pan-pan, jumps a tiger pit, rolls when it lands.

His right pulls the blinds.

His left lets one rip.

His right touches the keys like fruit
checked for ripeness by a football team.

His left stops in its tracks and shivers,
having found a corpse in the hedge.

His right shakes its moneymaker
at a nun, while his left

is held above the keys like a tongue
sickened by the fur of unbrushed teeth.

His right blames its parents and slams the door.

His left goes off its rocker, lets out
like a soccer match, crushing people in the stands.

His right is read the riot act while
his left sugars the sheriff's tank.

His right is winter, a pinhole of light broken open.

His left is a centaur having his way with a harpy
on top of the Golden Fleece.

His right thinks the garburator has turned
the left into a rosebud stump.

His left is flung on the guardrail like a car wreck.

His right turns back the tide.

His left is a combine going against the grain in the corn rows.

His right loves what you've done with your hair.

His left is a shut-in living through the eye in his door.

His right's limp as a severed gooseneck.

His left gives shelter to the poor, feels around
in the dark for someone it knows.

His right has nothing left to lose, so it brings home the bacon,
it spreads the threshold of your aorta while

the left is lowered by a long G chord
into the borehole of your heart.

MYSELF THE ONLY KANGAROO
AMONG THE BEAUTY
– *Emily Dickinson*

In the procession, wind farmers flutter
their hankies and the cellist's hand crabs
along the neck and the quayside flautist
foregoes gracenotes to watch the rowboat boys
come home and turn to stone and the tulip-fisted killer
knocks on the door of your eyesore and bows too quickly
as though his necktie caught the lathe and, bright enough,
he stands before the bulb and each day you get a piece
of that hostage in the mail and it was the time to kill
that he used unwisely, and after the shot animals stopped
and stillness groomed the grasslands and you thought
the phone on television was your own, and your daughter
is strapped to the pinwheel but he is so damn poor
at the knife throw and a megalith in a forgotten metropolis
has a toy flame in the frame of a paneless bay window
and the automobiles in the wrecking yard are autopsied
for trace amounts of conversation and he tells you love
is the Herculean task of being a janitor in an alabaster
abattoir and your lust is the carnivore
who's been at the back door five years
for the butterflies of those hinges to fly
open for you to wring the mop
into his baby bird mouth.

DICTAPHONE REEL OF GLENN GOULD'S
LAST GASP

The tune I wept to was dumbed down some
till it was a song I crept to while mulling over
swamp flats via the sticks, stumps and gangplanks.
I frogmarched from under a parasol pine.
Clouds parted and parts of the marsh
were stunned by a raygun sun.
The river's a sash, bashed in
by the alloy of starlight. Each leaf's
fallen-angel poise was chalked by the cops.
The lake's glass machinery stepped up a notch.
Rain like tape-hiss, lightning white as pineflesh.
I can see the bass-lipped Maria Callas, she has lashed
masts into a raft and is tossing up flares, strobing for me.
O Death, you threw me the axe while I was looking
at the sun, and each ivory I've dropped was a finger
clawing for the blufftop.

DEPTH OF FIELD

Uncoupling the Percherons,
you scrub a blush of white harness rot
with a pumice stone thumb. Their
horseshoe-crab hooves fossil the loam
moments before you tap a shell,
and one curls its foreleg so you can
hoofpick gravel from the frog.
Then we grasp the draft pole
and wheel the wagon hindfirst
into the driveshed.

Passing your monogrammed flask
like a baton, we watch the carpet grass.
Our backs slant like extra fence slats
on the fieldstone wall as an appaloosa
crests the esker and stalls. Tuberculoid thin,
woven in with the crimson sumac cobs,
we watch it awhile, then you tap your thumb
on your gutless flask before I can even ask
for one more haul. And still that appaloosa
stands. In its Rorschach-blotched hide we see
a sparrow pancaked on a bullet train's bow,
a pool of liquid iron ore from an ancient
meteor, a poof of smoke and a wizard's robes
pooled on the bootroom floor.

And still still that appaloosa stands
dousing us in stare. It won't even
starch an ear when the marl shifts
and twigs unstitch and a heap
of wolves thrush from the hawthorn
and milkweed twine, latching their canines
to its sheath, flank, hocks and forelock,

and pendulum on the crossbar of its jugular,
backflipping up on its swayback or scaling
its burr-crammed tail. That appaloosa
statues, wearing nothing but wolves.
Deadbolted to its esker as they break it down
blotch by blotch like a breadline on its last loaf
during the half-time of a long nuclear winter.

Then they blur away. You joggle your flask
for one last sip before we walk the glacial till
to its carcass, but there isn't. Its skeletal remains
lie like petrified trombones, whitened already
by sunups and white-noise wind. Ribs
rain-shuffled. No blood to speak of.

We got back to business shortly thereafter.
Noticing that we had lost ten years watching
that horse come apart. You had married, twice.
I had killed a man in Montreal. It all seemed so real.
Even the new police chief says so.

RAC•COON' *N.* —

A Middle Eastern dish with little to no raisins.

An island off Easter Island.

A transplanted organ stored at room temperature.

A shot in the dark.

A kind of parasol that Venus-flytraps you.

A vintage clown car.

A Gatling-type gun that will fire only on immediate relatives.

A sexual position favoured by the limbless.

A widow who rekindles old flames every other year.

A tepid lavender bath.

A virgin standing in the shadow of a failing crane.

The shy negotiation of leaves.

The angelical term for a supermodel's soul.

A Thai steamship that disappeared last week while on routine patrol.

MODULATED TIMBRE AND CADENCE FOR BABY GRAND

I resent the one-timeness, or the non-take-twoness,
of the live concert experience.
  – Glenn Gould

Wherever you go, you'll go by balloon
so as not to ruin the footprints
of your loved ones. You'll hand-shade
your eyes as you pilot your lighter-than-air
craft, making pylons of the factory stacks.
Balletic birds will crumple the quiet
with a conniption of trills over your lofting
bladder of boiled draft. By the seashore,
you'll see an octopus catcher plug his trident
into the beach as an abandoned bathysphere
pitches and bobs like last night's last pub dancer.
Downwind, two lovers will breathe in the cave
of a capsized dory, beneath the squall that will soon
toss your hand-blown bulb and basket off course,
touching it down on a crop-circled bull's eye,
a hork's distance from the rehearsal hall.
The audience inside will plant chairs
on your pant cuffs, pin you at the piano,
force you to spur a quarter horse through
their veins. You will be the Oppenheimer
of their senses, packed pews appraising the tattered
atoms your hands have become. Melodies flypapered
to the ditty-box of their souls. Your arms hollow sticks
stones rattle in, the crowd's clap's chloroform, as you
tear yourself from your gale-stripped chair
and step through the last reverberations
of the baby grand's tintinnabulations.

People who get their rocks off
in glass houses are the same people
who'd bend you over a rain barrel
just to give you the wet T-shirts
off their backs. You can't shoot
your mouth off if you're out of earshot.
Let bylaws be bygones, don't mind
your own business into the ground,
all that glitters is not cold to the touch.
You're only human once. If you've taken
the American way down a one-way street,
you've got to wipe your nose with the heart
on your sleeve. Don't knock yourself up over it,
baby. When they kicked dirt in your eye
they didn't think they'd be losing ground.
If your household name's ruined by word
of mouth, take the gift horse to town for a night
it won't soon forget. Colonel Sanders didn't lick
his fingers to the bone just so you could go it alone.
If you get what I'm getting at, raise your red hand.
You've got to kiss a lot of ass to get a little behind
in this business. Playing your silver spoons
with a bedpan band is like going for broke
at a church bazaar, more need than bother, more
clutch than grasp. You've got to be half in the bag
all the way to the bank. The mind is a terrible thing
to keep chaste. If you can't be drawn to my quarters,
do I part the sea and split? I treat my objects like women,
but I'm as Oedipal as you are Eve. True, I'd drop
a latch-key kid off at an open-cast mine,
but you're nothing to shake champagne at.
I think you'll agree with me here, the lake's
so clear you can see yourself to the door.

With a tall Tanqueray I watch the tornado footage:
aerials bent to mantis elbows while the corn rows rose –
each stock and cob, tiny rockets that shot to clog
God's forefinger as it gutted the lowlands.

5:04 a.m. and the telephone bring
brings the hues of Caleb's inhale, a flashlight's tusk
through the tobacco kiln's dark:
'Jeramy, something's landed out back.'

By full dawn I'm at the reveal:
an automobile in a field,
an F-150 King Cab covered with kelp.
This far inland, that chassis is all we know
about the Kraken. In the right light,
the invisible ink of Andromeda's palm
on the passenger's side pane.

The mother of Pearl shuffles in her boiled wool
petticoat. Pearl is fifteen. She is, how should I say.

In a white chemise coloured by chest wounds
he eats crystallized fruit while two hebelettes
steady a reed fan. The leper's gourd fists
pound like cracked heeltaps.

The sea-ghouls flying overhead say,
'Things in a language we never understand.'

The disease where no one appreciates you
was rampant. At that time, Pearl made a living
gathering crutches from altars
once miracles took root.

His muscular head in the blinkers
of her thighs. Pearl's tiny breasts
are tidy beasts flush to their egg's wall.
Her crease, a flared nostril.

Napoleon, as she slid her petals over him,
gained fresh respect for the ill, confessing,
'In the land of women who come
only when they're on top,
the bedridden man is king.'

A WINTER NIGHT

after Tomas Tranströmer

A child rigged like a cormorant
tugged our boathouse days
from their points of splendour.
Or strapped to a jetpack, perhaps.

A young lady puts her mouth
to the house. Both loathe the clamps
that keep the season tight over sounds
of ice shavings that teeter down like ash.
There is paper on the hills, it is winter.

When you return from the factory
where you fabricate the ash,
you trawl your dark room
for a switch on the wall

but your hand touches another face,
brushes another face. And you can't
remember the last time you felt like this
in the dark for something on the wall.

The streets flooded by people watching an apartment fire.
The Ku Klux white dress she wore. The weather's rigmarole.
The silver hero in the clouds. The galvanizing. The franchise.
The bright backwash. The hollow village. The weather's rebuttal.
The throat-cut rooster, its beak wide with crow.
The mule train bringing a piano through scrub brush.
The dwarf pines. The winterkill. The birch knots in the stove.
The waft as souvenir. The ripe lanterns in the orchard.
The crinoline lakes. The drowned lollystick legs.
The fishnets. The doldrums. The wanderlust. The Duchess.
The gramophone's tin ear. The carriage road.
The leaf mould. The unexploded ordinance. The bloom.
The small-arms fire. The child fire. The sightlines.
The dooryard. The courtlight. The wraith-sparrows.
The swagger. The little something to cut the dust.
The carbines. The Admiral's niece in oilskins.
The understudy who runs away with his wife.
The regency. The deadweight. The bedside telephone.
The stairs down the bluffs. The Empress on the pebble beach.
The moulting snakes. The wildfowl. The caverns.
The names run down by their echo.
The piano so immaculate it must be hollow.
The hawthorn belt around her muslin dress.
The jackdaws. The peck horns. The silverfish.
The dust-dulled brass. The rabbit-punch.
The wicker traps. The overcoat gone to seed.
The boozy weave of a grackle off the pane.
The cavalcade along her legs. The coronation.
The cannonade of hailstones on the xylophones.
The pterodactyl of silence that follows.

We handed in our weapons of self-destruction
to the mothers of the accused, we were chased
off the lake by the crooked elbows of a thousand
swimmers, carnival strippers met us at the shore,
we beached our boat by the book, tied it to a
whalebone horse hitch and continued contort-
ing through the woods bumping into shadow
foragers, gleaners in their bird-wing bras, they
brought us to the very brink.

That night, we slept under a tree bowed over
by lanterns, we woke in a Slovenian bathhouse,
Paganini played all through a breakfast of pin
cherries and pemmican, I saw the silver sequins
of semen on his trousers, I went so far as to say
I'm sorry, he put a brooch on your breast and
pointed us away, we had nothing to drop so
dropped our gaze instead, on the hill we looked
through the pay-per-view telescope and saw the
earth-sized storm on Neptune, when the gods
looked back I felt like a cardboard silhouette
standing suddenly at a rifle range, we don't ever
talk about it, it gets passed from memory to
memory by a language of mentioning, birds
come to perch on my jutting deformities, they
take flesh back to their mistress at the
leprosarium, a crowbar is the only tool named
after a bird.

We slept that night like puppies in a sack
tied to a tailpipe, we woke in bed with your
father, his bedside book is a catalogue of
sleepshapes, I tell him everything, whispering in
his one wind-deaf ear, he rises like a glider towed

to air by running men, you get dressed in paper-shredder strips and dance by the open hearth, when the radio wanes you sway to the static instead, I ask after the nerve gas of your perfume, you say my eyes have fallen in the oil-paint cracks of a portrait we picked off the bin, the glass coffee table looks like a scalped puddle, you come in and slit your shin on the corner, I can hear Pamplona bulls slipshod on the cobble as they run to fit through the red cape of your wound.

That night, the wind stopped and everyone fell over, but by and by we slept quite well in the hail-pocked greenhouse, woke back-to-back, pistols in hand on the dusty street, it began to rain so I heroically cut head holes in garbage bags, we shook the revolutionary's pamphlet hands, we bent to pet the dogs in our periphery, they writhed like Pope John Paul under a lap dancer, we went off half-mocked by the passersby, we ran, firing over our shoulders, as the pitchfork mob grew randier by the second, we had to depart in a cart drawn by swans, we dropped the reins and gave them their head, at roadside motels we let their lips comb our timbered armhairs, they made their way on our splayed limbs, at each waterway we laid our capes on the creek and crossed arm in arm, we learnt the lake lore, we tied a dental-floss leash to the tussock moth, it led us to the cuticle moon, the bent cob of moon racked on its hook, its reflection of pearl divers cat-curled on the sea bottom.

That night, we slept among the lumber-camp legends calm as a mill pond, we woke to one white carriage moving at a pedophile's pace through the doused streets, we baked razors into our bread, we brought loaves to the prisoners, they let the guards live, killing themselves instead, in our off-hours we calibrated the gradient of the slope to forgetting, we calculated the half-life of love, we got snagged on semantics, we war-cried through the entire ceremony, we bottled the breeze-path of fainting brides, all the flushed fish came back to life and swung themselves into the distance.

We slept that night on a raft in a rain pond pooled on a flat-roofed factory, we woke on the weather-wet side of the barn, from here we sailed on a sea under the soil, last of the ground-water corsairs, we cried behind the backs of the dead, above us magicians stopped mid-trick as you bathed in the crosshatch of rain, halted, we heard the pat of a windfall apple, in the distance the varicose of flashlights waved in the woods, an accordion pulled its last breath, in this bottleneck of the woods we are as rare as a photograph of cloud tops, we rise to watch cattle renovate the landscape between a litter of barn carcasses, a dark rider crosses the moon-clobbered field cupping the slop of his cud-chewn heart, we shake the fever loose and huddle near the barnfire, in the dark farmhouse flies lie on the banks of the insectivorous windowsills, outside deer drift like flies at the pond's window, there is no country tonight, the thickets are slit and there is enough distance to break your eye open, we sang till the killdeers fell on their own swords, we plucked the lighthouse jewel, tore the tickbird from the clock, we consulted a stable of doctors, they told us a wolf is a wolf is a wolf and he will take us, before we slept that night you balmed your lips and I sat at a baby grand, farmers shuffled in, sombre as flies downed by rain, but by the end of our fierce duet they had turned quickly brittle again.

At night we mimed our way out of that mess, we slept on the lam, out on a limb, we woke ditchside on the whale road, the sea was a lunatic lashed to bed rails, we lit lights to lure lost ships, we said what the conch shells always said, let us two be the Sutton Hoos of this beach we reached through a clamour of clam mouths, I believe in music, the fraying mouth of coat sleeves, the bulrushes' hackled lean, I know you do too, my companion ruffled by the wince of hammered strings, a Valkyrie is seesawing towards us, broadaxe in hand, and in that moment you flapped from me I could picture a thousand words I wanted to say to make you stay.

The poem 'Happy Birthday, Carl Linnaeus, 300 Years Old' is a found poem that has been slightly altered from a pamphlet of the same name.

'Second Glance at Corrag' is after the Ted Hughes poem 'Second Glance at a Jaguar.' In this case I had the German shepherd Corrag, of Corrag Mean, in mind.

'The Official Translation of Ho Chi Minh's August 18th, 1966, Telephone Call' has been 'transliterated' from so-called CIA cassette tapes of a wire-tap I bought over the Internet. As far as I know, none of the lines are accurate translations of the Vietnamese; however, they are true to cadences in the recorded speech.

The italicized line in 'Sable Island Concertina, Circa 1887' is from Charlie Smith's poem 'As for Trees.'

'Rabbit' is for Inger Bråtveit.

'Père Joseph and the Bush Cord' is after a character created by Joshua Trotter. The poem is a tribute to both of them.

'Depth of Field' is for Tim Hallowell.

'Sunrise with Seamonster' is after Joseph Mallord William Turner's painting of the same name.

'Napoleon in the Plague House at Jaffa' is after Baron Antoine-Jean Gros's painting *Napoleon Bonaparte Visiting the Victims of the Plague at Jaffa, 11 March 1799*, 1804.

'Glenn Gould Negotiates the Danube in the Company of a Raven' is loosely based on the Romani myth and song, usually titled 'A Stork Crosses the Danube, in the Company of a Raven.' I had the Taraf de Haïdouks' performance in mind while working on the poem. The poem is a 'translation' of Glenn Gould's recording of Bach's Chromatic Fantasy in D Minor (BWV 903). Using an invented, baroque and highly suspect form of hieroglyphics and/or tablature, I have attempted to translate the fugue into English. My apologies to Johann Sebastian Bach, Mr. Gould, Taraf de Haïdouks and the reader.

Thank you to the staff, faculty and participants of the Banff Centre for the Arts, Writers Studio 2004, especially Don McKay who edited an earlier version of this manuscript. Thank you to the Baltic Centre for Writers and Translators in Visby, Sweden, and the Centre for Writers and Translators in Rhodes, Greece, for residencies that allowed me to work on some of these. And to the Kent Farndale Bursary, the Ontario Arts Council and the Canada Council for the Arts for their financial support.

Arc, Capilano Review, Event, The Fiddlehead, Grain, Prism International, Syd & Shirley, Upstairs at Duroc (France), *Journal Des Poètes* (Belgium), *Vārti* (Latvia), *Ateneu* (Romania) and *Blá a Handklæ ið* (Iceland), have published earlier versions of some of these poems – praise to the editors and translators. Thanks also to littlefishcartpress, which published the chapbook *Winter Horse and Other Poems* and the anthology *This Grace*. Selections of poems from this collection received the 2006 Bronwen Wallace Memorial Award and the 2007 CBC Literary Award and were published in *enRoute* magazine.

So much has depended upon Anna Kaarina Koskinen. And Caleb and Eli Robinson, Aaron Shannik and Tim Hallowell. And Gordon Johnston, Margaret Steffler, Zach Gaviller, John Climenhage, Barry Dempster, Ingrid Ruthig, Sharon McCartney, Matthew Tierney and Zachariah Wells for their friendships and discussions. Thank you to Stephanie Noble and to Ben and Pat Noble. To Lawrence Jackson. To Wally and Jo Horniak. And Lára Þórarinsdóttir. To Cameron 'Clammy' Esler. To Stephanie Boddington for her support and knowledge of the secret scattered docksides of our Eastern Ontarian Empire. A special thanks to Kevin Connolly for getting these properly primped and perfumed. And to Alana Wilcox, Christina Palassio, Evan Munday and the rest of the folks at Coach House for getting them all to the ball. Much grace to my parents, John and Janie Dodds. My love to Brecken Rose Hancock. And all to Joshua Trotter, Leigh Kotsilidis and Gabe Foreman, for their spiritual, existential, metaphorical and editorial guidance.

Jeramy Dodds lives in Orono, Ontario. He is the winner of the 2006 Bronwen Wallace Memorial Award and the 2007 CBC Literary Award in poetry. He works as a research archaeologist.

Typeset in Adobe Caslon
Printed and bound at the Coach House on bpNichol Lane

Edited by Kevin Connolly
Designed by Alana Wilcox
Cover image, *Monsters that Walk the Earth* (coloured pencil, 16" x 28",
   2007) by Michael Krueger (michaelkrueger.us), used with the
   permission of the artist

Coach House Books
401 Huron Street on bpNichol Lane
Toronto, Ontario M5S 2G5

416 979 2217
800 367 6360

mail@chbooks.com
www.chbooks.com